Pocket Book of Madness

AF623657

Heather Sinclair

BookLeaf Publishing

Presentation by *BookLeaf Publishing*

Web: www.bookleafpub.com

E-mail: info@bookleafpub.com

ISBN: 9789357212847

First edition 2023

PREFACE

Although not cheerful in nature
I'd be willing to wager
These poems and rhymes
Will all but define
The ramblings of this total stranger

It's All In My Head

But it's all in my head.

A thought that fought so hard not to be
Becomes a parasite in my mind that I can't help but mother
Covering the vast distance between us with baby steps of mammoth proportions
Leaving chasms in their wake

My heart hurts for what's here
And what never will be
A silent riot under a pensive surface that,
I beg, please don't break
Because I'm too fragile

Torn to pieces by paths of impossible probabilities
Or improbable possibilities
I don't know, and I can't allow myself to want to know
But I do
And I don't
And I...

But it's all in my head, yeah?

In you hearing this now
I'm crying out for you to please understand.
For the words to somehow get under your skin
so that you know without knowing the words
that I'm not speaking
Because I might have many different faces
But I can't face those

And I can't hold you to the weight of my
expectations
Or at all for that matter
I shouldn't want to
But I do
And I don't
And I...

But it's all in my head

I've created you
I've moulded you into an image of myself
A damaged, broken soul
Clawing out
Aching for something that you can't have
And I can't either.
That person doesn't exist,
But all I want is for you to tell me that they do.

The shackles that hold me back from you are also the feathers in the pillow that absorb my tears at night
My safety is all that I know
And suddenly it's not so safe at all.

The feathers scratch at my skin
And I push them away
Only to be smothered.
Engulfed in a suffocating normalcy
Within which I can't falter
I can't fail
Because I hold myself to such high standards
But in such low regard

The only energy that I had left
Now not a spark, but a sodden wick.
Heavy and useless
I wish I had the energy to fight
And I do
But I don't
And I...

But It's all in my head, right?

My head that's full of bees by day
And when I wipe the honey from my nose
I try to hide it but it's too much

My hands stick to everything I touch as I try to steady myself
The loose links of my knees have no power against gravity

Until by night there's only one left and it's you
The pit in my head
Vast and empty but for the walls stacked high with compressed thoughts and fears and loves and lies and you
Right there in the middle
The perfect atmosphere for you to echo

You can't be here
Do you even know that you are?

Or is it all in my head?

Canticum Sirenis

Hindsight is a siren
Singing beautiful memories
Strung with nostalgia.
Reconstructing them
To fit the metre,
She calls you to remember
How she sees fit.

Dropping details
Like missed notes in a chord.
Slowing the tempo.
Forcing emphasis upon phrases -
The ones she wants you to hear -
You're drawn to the sound
With an urgent hunger.

But she eludes you.
Evasive as a name
On the tip of your tongue,
Belonging to a face you cannot place -
The melody plays in your mind
But you cannot recreate it,
Try as you might.

You map the sounds
As they reverberate
In the cavernous wells,
But you can't decipher the notes -
And still she sings to you.
You salivate at the thought
Of the next verse.

A cappella, she calls
In sharps and flats
But never in minor key,
Less she call back a tragedy.
Only hoping you pursue
The cadence that once
Held your attention.

Impossible to catch,
The feeling in that moment -
Not the one you heard
But the stories that it called upon -
Dredging them through years
Of insignificant moments
And pointless analogies

So you chase her -
Like a dream, she fades
In and out,
Only catching the end of a chorus
You latch on and claw at it,

Desperate to remember
What you once so longed to forget.

Soot & Debris

I want these emotions to be yours.

I long for the sadness to be fleeting
And the dread to be softenable.
For the well in my chest
To be fillable
With your love alone,
But they're not.
It's not.

When I say
I want these emotions to be yours,
I don't mean that I want you to hurt
Or have hurt me.
I mean that I want them to be fixable by you,
But despite the warmest glow
And the indescribable love that you show me,
They can't be.

You didn't put them there
So you can't dismantle them
Or the shelves that hold them in place.
How could you possibly know where to start?
How could you know which piece to lift first

Without fear of the stacks tumbling down on top of you,
On top of me,
And trapping us there.

I can't entomb you in them with me.
I need you on the outside
Shining the light
Guiding me to the surface,
But to do that - you must first reach the top.

How can I ask that of you?
How can I expect you to shred your palms on the ascent
And risk piercing your bones if you lose your footing?

I don't want you to look at them.
They're not yours,
They're not for you,
And the fact that they still occupy so much space in my heart and mind
Feels like a betrayal.

I want these emotions to be yours
So that I can sob into your shoulder
And have you comfort me

Without feeling like I'm going to shatter
something fragile.
The knowledge that what we have is
indestructible
Doesn't negate the fact that you, yourself are not.

How could I live with myself
If you changed anything at all
Because of something I said
That I can't change.
I need to protect you from this
I need to cushion you from the waves that
emanate from my scorched heart
That still ebbs with the dying heat of an old
flame -
Desperate to shake it off
But still having pieces crumble to ash from years
of unevenly stoked fires.

I need to fix this myself,
And scrubbing the soot from the walls
Will be harder than expected
When there's a new inferno.

Names

I didn't consent to this.
I didn't subscribe
To the idea that names can have weight
And that I'd have to carry them
Like shoulder pad bricks -
Every new issue being stacked and cemented -
Until I turn my head and all I see are walls.

Without a name,
I can pretend.
I can make believe that the bricks are reels of film -
Light shining through the negatives
But never processing.

But if I turn away,
The back of my head becomes a canvas.
The light burns through into the fibres
And darkens them
Until it's all I see.

So I call it by name,
And it rears its ugly head and looks me right in the eye.
I'm there

Staring at my own reflection
And it's heavy -
It's so God-damned heavy.

The name takes a seat at the table on my chest
And adds pressure.
Names ask for action -
They insist upon it -
But I'm just not strong enough.

I'm collecting them now.
Filling that table
In the hopes that the weight crushes my lungs
Before I have to concede to their requests.

Reversal

In this game of cat and mouse
I'm running scared all through the house
Calculating where you'll pounce
And how your win will be announced

But next time I will strategize
And I will take the biggest prize
Yet no-one cares a single ounce
When I'm the cat and you're the mouse.

Let Go

Letting go of a future
Is the hardest thing to do
The past is left behind us
But I let go of that, too

That was a little easier
I can say that much is true
Because the past already happened
And we just about pulled through

That doesn't mean to say
That I'm trying to undo
All those years we spent together
Throughout which we both grew

But letting go of a future
Is the hardest thing to do
Because letting go of a future
Means I'm letting go of you.

Breathe

A sideways glance or a hushed whisper
Or a "vibe" that just feels off
Becomes a pit in a stomach or a stone lodged in a throat
And, unwittingly, a trigger is pulled.
There's no stopping the frantic, panicked sprint
Down staircases spiralling into the dark.
Suddenly, the glances are sneers
And the whispers are an onslaught of jibes.

Vibrating numbness ebbs from fingertip to forearm
Lungs, concrete slabs
Unmoving and unwilling to receive and deliver
A sinking rush, combusting
Overflowing yet painfully contained
Begins to catastrophise
Until the tongues of flames tickle even the most fleeting of thoughts

Dizzying moments feel like hours and days
And physical darkness calls to comfort
The waves of hyperventilation that are all the concrete allows
The space, a reminder of safety

A reminder of simplicity and empty mind
It beckons.
Sit here until it finally arrives.
Everything is fine.

The Hardest Goodbye

I've said goodbye to you a hundred times
And another thousand in my head
But I've only had to endure the pain a few times
Of holding you close
Gripping the fabric covering your back
As if the woven threads could somehow convey
My aching need for you to stay

Holding a little too tight
For a little too long
Never wanting to be the one to break away
Because the space created when I do
Always feels like lightyears

Winded by the way my heart sticks
To the underside of your chest
As it's ripped from my own.
Watching the beating slow
As you turn your back and leave with it.
My lungs can never function without it in those moments
And my throat closes around the words:

"Come Back"

She

The face you see before you
I swear she isn't me
She covers all emotion
And masks off the unseen

A noble strong protector
She filters all my thoughts
Knows all the strengths and weaknesses
Of demons that I've fought

She's memorized these creases
And crevices of mine
That map across my forehead
She's learned of every line

She's siphoned off my memories
Distorted frames of time
She's taken all the good parts
So they don't feel like they're mine

She plasters on a smile each day
And takes on all appointments
She powers through them deftly
But takes all the enjoyment

See, the girl that stands before you
I swear she isn't me
She's just the me I need to be
To get through days like these.

[Pro/Re]act

We are all reactive
Even on the days that we have no energy to react
An empty vessel with absorbent skin
We try to allow the waves to crash over
But we take it all in
We take it all onboard
And we react

A bullet ricochets on the inside
Breaking us down
Wearing the walls away
Crack after crack
But we wake up the next morning
And react.
We make that unconscious decision to heal
And we go on.

We can't be proactive
The future is the unknown behind every corner
With no way of knowing whether we'll be
engulfed in light
Or drowned in darkness
We can learn
We can plan
But ultimately

What do we do but use the plans and knowledge
To react?

So that's how it goes
That's what we do.
We take it all
Soak it up
Or push it away
We consume and we respond.

We react.

Palate Cleanser

You keep me warm.
I'm at home. It's early in the evening.
You arrive - and give me the warmest of hugs.

You keep me safe.
On the mornings when I'm not quite awake,
You build me up - enough that I can get to work on time.

You keep me sane.
I'm at work - having a stressful day.
You surprise me - and give me the strength to reach 6 o'clock.

You are my drug.
Quite literally, in every way.
I don't think I can live without you.
I wouldn't dare try.

You are my favourite part of the day.
My sweet caffeine.
My dark, bitter Americano.
My coffee.

Weeks 1 Through Seven

I'll fill each day with laughter
And I'll play my favourite songs
I'll write using my free time
And I'll paper all my walls
I'll decorate the living room
And give my friends a call
But the first thing I must do
Is learn to live all on my own

I'll text your mum and ask her
How she's getting on at work
I'll do a load of laundry
And I'll package up your shirts
I'll spend a little free time
Playing word games on my phone
But the first thing I must do
Is learn to live all on my own

I'll keep myself real busy
And I'll buy logs for the fire
I'll paint my toenails purple
And I'll sleep when I get tired
I'll look at all the cats online
That I know I can't home
But the first thing I must do

Is learn to live all on my own

I'll think about how things have changed
And how they could have been
I'll ponder over words unsaid
And sights we left unseen
I'll try my best to forget
That we both are now alone
But the first thing I must do
Is learn to live all on my own

Onion

I can't with this.
It's like I'm in a perpetual state of falling
Following a corkscrew of absolute madness
That everyone else thinks is normality

I'm happy to talk about it
Well, not happy. Not even content.
But it's the done thing, isn't it?
I feel like people expect me to talk
And if I didn't I'd be odd

It'd be like going through a huge life event
And telling no-one.
That's really what it is
But I make light of it.
I only tell what would already be known from the outside
Because that's the only layer I can pull off

Another layer, and I'm vulnerable
I have to show my insecurities despite my strengths.
I have to admit that I'm not the rock that I'm expected to be
I'm not solid

I'm liquid - vibrating in the depths of the
unknown.

Another layer and I'm raw
And that's not pretty.
Nobody wants to see the red underneath the
calm pallor of skin

But that's me.
I am the red. I am the mess.
And whether or not I become the phoenix rising
from the ashes
I will still take the ashes over any other facade
of life.

Because I can't with this. But I can.
And I will.

I Paint My Nails

I paint my nails so that I don't bite them
Only instead, I pick at my skin.
In meetings, I thoughtlessly circle
The soft space between my earlobe and neck
Wearing it down.
My fingertips that drafted countless emails
Just as abrasive then as they are now.
Pushing past the heat
They continuously circle
Until they draw blood.

I paint my nails so that I don't bite them
Only instead, I bite my lips.
The small pieces of dry skin
Brought on by the onslaught of a harsh winter
Nibbled away and discarded
Like the hundreds of tasks procrastinated over
But never finished.
Chewing at the muscles
That convey the most basic emotions on my
face.

I paint my nails so that I don't bite them
Only instead, I rub my eyes.
Forcing stars to shoot across

My focus, now devoid of any vision
I watch them dance
Taking my attention from reality and forcing it
Into my own head
Tears stream
And even bloodshot, I don't cease.

I paint my nails so that I don't bite them
Only instead, I bounce my legs.
A vibrating discontent
It shakes the table and its contents
A kinetic agitation
That looks outwardly absurd
And uncomfortable
The pressure on my feet
Causing a movement I can't stop.

I paint my nails so that I don't bite them
Only instead, I question myself.
My own harshest critic
I call upon my shortcomings.
My red, flaking skin highlighting my nervous composure
And worrisome habits
And I wonder
If I should stop painting my nails?

Woven

I loop and I knot
And I bring the fabric together upon itself
Like a memory, it comes back.
It always comes back
Until it's entirely woven into the body of my
design.

A textile version of myself.
Forwards and backwards, always repeating
myself.
Sometimes repeating the same mistakes - just to
be sure
That they were mistakes in the first place
And not a result of coincidence and misfortune.

Mostly a project of repetition in most cases.
Not to reach an end result.
My project has no real end.
I just knit to pass the time
My rows are my weeks
My ends are beginnings
And my project is time itself.

Islands

The rain pours as my flight lands
A stark reminder of the differences between life with and without you
And a cruel promise to continue reminding me
Whilst I hail a taxi home.

Home. Such an empty word when you're not here.
As empty as my arms feel
Only hours after they were wrapped around you.

The weight sits heavy on my chest
As a sigh releases the last of the wings which hatched in its walls each time
I was there to hear you say my name.

If "Hello" lasts a week
"Goodbye" stretches and suffocates Two.
I struggle to muster the Me that's here when you're not
When molehills become mountains and you've taken my shoes.

Echoes

A life echoes in time forever
In ways that both can and cannot be measured

A life ended is measured in the grief of those that love
It's measured in the tempered smiles and hushed laughter
Brought on by the memories of a life lived

It's measured in the loss felt by those left behind
The absence of being. The missing line in a song.
The joy brought to a halt by the void that once was full.

The warmth that was felt is now only a lingering memory
Of arms round your shoulders on a rough day
Or a voice praising your strength after a job well done.

The echo reverberates and stings to your core
In a bittersweet, joyous recall of a soul that once was

The reason you got up in the morning, even if
you didn't know it.

But it can't be measured at all
As it's so much more.

The life left behind is you
In every way that you were guided and taught
In lessons that you didn't know needed learning.

Its in the simplest of smiles
Received by a stranger on the edge
That continued on to be something

Anything, in the sense that they continued to be
And that was down to that one second in time
Because life is made up of many seconds.

Seconds turn to hours
And hours turn to days
And days continue until they're replayed as an
echo in someone elses story.

So you will be measured
But your legacy will not.
But do not fret, as the immeasurable will be
measured in memory.

I'm There

My heart escapes from my chest
My lungs struggle
And my mind goes wild

You're there

A million thoughts race through my head
My heart breaks again
And my veins pulse in fear

You're there

I can't describe the irrationality
The understanding that it's not real
And yet the knowledge that

You're there

It gives me strength in the knowledge
That I'm not alone
And that I can be me

So,
Unfiltered
Unaltered
Unscreened

You're there

And yet

Your heart escapes from your chest
Your lungs struggle
And your mind goes wild

Let me be there

A million thoughts race through your head
Your heart breaks again
And your veins pulse in fear

Let me be there

You can't describe the irrationality
The understanding that it's not real
And yet the knowledge that

I want to be there

I hope it gives you strength in the knowledge
That you're not alone
And that you can be you

So,
Unfiltered
Unaltered
Unscreened

I'm there

A Mirror's Reflection

The mirror sees what I want it to see
I've engineered it that way
No longer does it point and jeer
And put me down each day

For I am but a meat machine
Operated by a brain
But when I passed the glass before
It drove me quite insane

I'd see the things I didn't like
I'd wish them all away
Unhealthy thoughts commanded
And my days were cold and grey

So now I just remember
That a floating brain I am
And I feed myself the extra slice
Of tiger bread and jam

Extra pounds and folds and lines
My meat suit might be showing
But in my mind I know I'm me
And I'm positively glowing

The mirror sees what I want it to see
I've engineered it that way
Because I know now it's not at fault
And my reflection will stay.

Sleep It Off

You wake up
Make your morning coffee
And leave
Your car's engine light is showing
You sigh

Work is uneventful but generally shit
You come home and don't eat dinner

You've had a tough day
Sleep it off
You'll feel better in the morning

You wake up
Make your morning coffee
The engine light's still on
You sigh and catch your neighbor's eye
And give them a curt nod

Work is uneventful but generally shit
The car has a new noise on the drive home
You cook dinner and accidentally scald yourself
while pouring the water from the pan

You've had a tough day
Sleep it off
You'll feel better in the morning

You wake up
Drop your car at the mechanic
And take the bus
Someone sits next to you and you tense up
Trying desperately to avoid touching elbows
with a stranger less they realise you exist

Work is shit
You missed a deadline that had slipped your
mind
You go home and fish out the packet of
cigarettes you had stashed in the drawer when
you quit 2 years ago
You light one
It's dry and harsh

You've had a tough day
Sleep it off
You'll feel better in the morning

You wake up
You pick up the car
It leaves a 400 quid hole in your pocket
But it drives like new

Work is shit
It's just shit
You run a bath at home
And slip under the water
Holding your breath until your lungs burn
You shake your head at yourself when you
surface

You've had a tough day
Sleep it off
You'll feel better in the morning

You wake up
The coffee machine is clogged
You go to work

Work is shit
You sent a message to a friend on lunch
They didn't respond
On the drive home you wonder how long you
can close your eyes on the motorway
1
2
3...
A horrid laugh escapes you when you open them
You get home in one piece

You've had a tough day
Sleep it off
You'll feel better in the morning

You wake up
You can't face work so you call in

You sit in the living room and stare at the blank TV screen
The room is cold
The friend you messaged yesterday has left you on read
You decide against pushing it with a second message

You've had a tough day
Sleep it off
You'll feel better in the morning

You wake up
You don't go to work
The room is cold

You've had a tough day
Sleep it off
You'll feel better in the morning

You wake up
The room is cold
You wonder how many times the demons in your head will walk the same laps

You've had a tough day
Sleep it off
You'll feel better in the morning

You wake up
You realise you haven't cried in 2 months
Would it help?
You try but you can't
The room is cold

You've had a tough day
Sleep it off
You'll feel better in the morning

You wake up
The room is cold

You've had a tough day
Sleep it off

You wake up

You've had a tough day
Sleep it off

You wake up...

You find yourself in front of your medicine cabinet
You don't recognise yourself in the mirror
There are horrors in the hollows of your eyes
Your first turns the glass into sand
Why did you do that?

You've had a tough day
Sleep it off

Soon

Soon the sun will shine on me
And I'll know how it feels
To bask in it and soak it in
And allow myself to heal

www.ingramcontent.com/pod-product-compliance
Lightning Source LLC
Chambersburg PA
CBHW051741130826
49812CB00033B/947
9789357212847